Going
the Distance

My Run to the Son

by
Jerry Snider

Illustrated by
Kathleen Varn

eShore

Pittsburgh, PA

ISBN 1 - 58501- 024 - 3

Trade Paperback
©Copyright 2000 Jerry Snider
All rights reserved
First printing - 2000
Library of Congress # 99-65227

Request for information should be addressed to:

CeShore Publishing Co.
The Sterling Building
440 Friday Road
Pittsburgh, PA 15209
www.ceshore.com

CeShore Publishing Co. is an imprint of SterlingHouse Publisher, Inc.

Cover design: Steve Czarnecki - SterlingHouse Publisher, Inc.
Illustrations: Kathleen Varn
Photographer: Judy Morehead
Typesetting: Lucy Matyjaszczyk

Scripture quoted from
The New King James Version
The New Living Translator
The New International Version
Contemporary English Version

Printed in Canada

FOREWORD

by

Patricia Wingard Carson,

Author of *Peculiar Pain* and *The Wonderment.*

Going the Distance is a spiritual marathon that takes you to your higher self. Jerry Snider takes a physical foot race and parallels it with the journey of life we are required by birth to take part in. His unique and creative writing style gives life's journey depth and meaning. He makes complex spiritual principles simple and easy to understand. Like the master teacher, Jesus Christ, Jerry uses common happenings in our day to day lives to awaken our spirituality and encourage our positive participation in the game of life. He invites us to reevaluate our level of responsibility in our own spiritual growth.

Reading *Going the Distance* is a must for all who seek personal fulfillment and enlightenment on this journey of life. Mile after mile, Jerry reminds us of the blessings we so often take for granted and of the golden opportunities we so often overlook.

Going the Distance is a must for anyone who is on the pathway of purpose. Jerry gives us life's blueprint and reveals the ingredients for stamina and courage. *Going the Distance* challenges your inner greatness and reconnects you with your higher self.

Praise
for
Going the Distance

"There are books that run several hundred pages or come in several volumes, yet Jerry Snider's book, *Going the Distance*, speaks volumes in just over 100 pages.

Snider is a marathon runner who combines his running experiences, plus his unique wit and story-telling ability, with a positive Christian perspective to create 26.2 inspirational and entertaining stories. Jerry Snider's book is sure to become a permanent fixture in your library to read again and again not only to continue in helping you focus on the positive possibilities life has to offer, but to also show you that the only real certified course to follow in the marathon of life is to Run to the Son."

- Karl Gruber
Super Run for the Cure to benefit leukemia research.
Runner of 52 marathons in 52 weeks; May '96-April '97

"I'm a busy man and I hate to run. As a result of reading Jerry's book, I'm still busy but have found a refreshing challenge to persevere in whatever I attempt, even running. We all need a cheerleader. Jerry gives us that kind of encouragement with *Going the Distance.*"
- Jim Zuber
Senior pastor, Linworth Road Community Church

"Brilliant!! Very Inspirational!! Great Stories!! Heart-tugging!! Spirit-lifting!!" **- Amy Fault-Phillips**
Campaign manager for the Leukemia Society of America

"Delightful reading!! Written with lightheartedness, humor, and sincerity. Sends messages of faith, hope, encouragement to all who struggle through difficult times. A good example of how we all could (and should) witness to the little miracles we experience in our own run to the Son."
- Diane Byrd, Director
Ronald McDonald House, Columbus, Ohio

"Jerry has captured the essence of his humor, faith, and commitment to others in this book of short stories. The world shines brighter because Jerry cared enough to share his thoughts and childlike faith with the rest of us. His run is truly to the Son."
- Dan E. Steele
Steele Management, Inc., Medical Practice Management

Acknowledgements

I would like to acknowledge these people for their encouragement to keep running to and writing for the Son: Shannon Snider, Mom and Dad, Karl Gruber, Charlie and Marian McDaniel, Juliana Laufersweiler, Anita Bensonhaver, Gary Fidler, Dan and Carol Steele, Diane LeMay, Anita Temple, Becky Wollard, and Judith James.

Thank you,
Jerry

For Mom, whose encouragement has always been appreciated.

Love,
Kathleen

Dedicated to the memory of

Dr. Norman Vincent Peale

Table of Contents

Mile I
No Such Thing

*"The race is not to
the swift or the battle to
the strong."*
Ecclesiastes 9:11

Legless Vet Finishes Marathon. I read the news in the fall of 1986, just one week before I was to run in the Columbus Marathon for the first time.

The man they were talking about is Bob Wieland, a born-again Christian. Accompanying the story was a photograph of Bob at the finish line of the New York Marathon with a race number pinned to his chest, his arms stretched overhead in a victory pose and a smile spread across his face. The people captured in the background of the picture were applauding.

Bob Wieland was forty years old when he finished the New York Marathon. Seventeen years earlier, he was serving as an army medic in the jungles of Vietnam. During the heat of battle, while working to save the wounded, he stepped on a mine. His legs went in one direction and his upper body in another. He was given little chance of survival. The possibility that Bob would someday run in a marathon was probably the last thing his doctors would have predicted.

There were 19,413 runners who finished the New York Marathon in 1986 and Bob Wieland came in last-or did he?

"Success is not based on where you start," Wieland said. "It's where you finish- and I finished."

Several years ago, when my daughter, Shannon, was in middle school, she struggled with the subject of science. She was moved to a special class-at least, I called it "special." Shannon had another name for it.

"Dad," she said, "you know I'm in the dumb class for science."

"There is no such thing as a dumb class," I told her and then added, "or a slow race."

Thinking of Bob, and my own first marathon, I reminded my daughter that she had watched me and several thousand other people run the Columbus Marathon.

"All the runners out there were running the same race with the same goal. However, we all crossed the finish line at different times. We all did the best we could."

There was silence as we hugged. "Someone once told me that God didn't expect me to be *the* best," I continued my pep talk. "God expected me to be *my* best."

Bob Wieland ran his race in a sitting position, using his powerful arms to lift his body and swing it forward on a fifteen pound saddle. He called the pads he wore over clenched fists, "size-one running shoes."

Moving at an average speed of one mile per hour, it took him four days, two hours, forty-eight minutes, and seventeen seconds to finish the race. It was called the slowest time in marathon history.

A week later, I finished my first marathon in five hours. In spirit, I ran with Bob Wieland. I felt more like a tortoise than a hare that day. What kept me going was Bob Wieland's words at the end of his marathon: "The first step was the most difficult. After that, we were on our way home . . . the joy has been the journey."

I don't know how long my daughter remembered our conversation about her "special" class. I can tell you that, eventually, she conquered middle school science and numerous other subjects. She walked across the stage of the high school audi-

2

torium on June 5, 1994, to receive her diploma and it all began with a single step.

The first step . . . the joy . . . the journey. That's what the *Going the Distance: My Run to the Son* is all about.

Mile 2
Running from the Neck Up

*"But they that wait
upon the Lord shall renew
their strength; they shall
mount up with wings as eagles;
they shall run and not
be weary, and they shall
walk and not faint."*
Isaiah 40:31

Each fall, thousands of spectators line the streets of Columbus, Ohio, and neighboring communities to watch runners challenge, charge, drag, stumble, and push themselves to the finish line of the 26.2 mile Columbus Marathon. I have completed the race eleven times.

Every year, about a week before the race, I start a campaign to collect the autographs of family and friends on the shirt I'll be wearing in the race. The shirt always has a picture of an eagle and a reference to Isaiah 40:31.

With a laundry marker that boasts of being indelible, people sign their names and then add their favorite Bible verses, affirmations, slogans, or graffiti. Among my favorites have been:

- Right foot, left foot-a lot
- With determination comes success
- I can do all things through Christ who strengthens me
- Run like you stole something
- Winners get up, losers give up
- Be in the light
- I can + I will = I did!
- See you at the finish line

There have been so many it would take a whole book just to list them. Perhaps my favorite was accompanied by a picture of feet. Beside the feet were the words, "The thrill of victory and the agony of de feet."

Remember, I said the marathon is 26.2 miles long. *Webster's Dictionary* defines a marathon as "a long distance race, an endurance contest". If we agree with Webster, then everyone has a marathon race to run. It may not be a foot race through the streets of Columbus, Chicago, Boston, New York, or some other city, but a situation that calls for courage, hope, and perseverance. I call this "running from the neck up."

One friend who signed my shirt was a prisoner of war in North Vietnam for five years. That would certainly qualify as a marathon. Another whose name appears on my shirt has spent her whole life in a wheelchair. Other names belong to people whose marathon consists of fighting the addictions of alcohol and drugs. Being parents of handicapped children, victims of abuse, or delinquent teenagers-they've all signed their names.

On race day, I don my shirt filled with signatures and words of encouragement. Other runners have referred to me as "the guy with the John Hancock shirt". Most people think it's a great idea.

To me, it's far more than just a collection of names. Almost every situation a human being is capable of finding himself or herself in is represented on my race day shirt.

6

As I think about my friends the situations they have been in, everything they are going through now, or what they have survived I pray for each one. Life is not a quick and easy sprint. It's a marathon. *Keep running to the Son.*

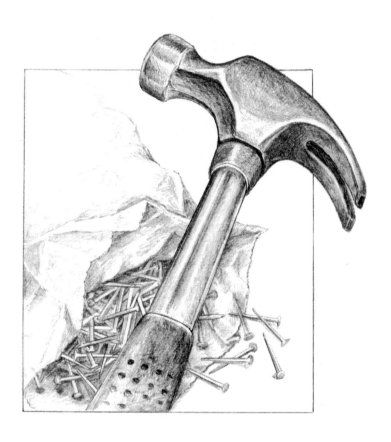

Mile 3
Hammer and Nails

*"This one thing I
do, forgetting those things
which are behind and
reaching forth unto those
things which are before
us."*
Philippians 3:13

The piercing echo of sirens and the howling of my dog, Lady, shattered the silence of a restful sleep. I fumbled for a light switch as I rubbed my eyes. It was after midnight.

The sirens blared louder now and an instant later, flashing lights were dancing through the curtains of my window.

"Quiet, Lady, quiet," I said to the dog as I reached for my glasses.

I could feel my heart pounding faster now as I looked out the window at a street full of fire engines, their crews moving quickly to position hoses and ready ladders.

The house directly across the street was almost fully engulfed in flames. Neighbors were charging out of their houses, pulling on jackets and robes as they moved. I quickly dressed, put a leash on the dog, and joined the group stationed in front of my house. Word got around: Everyone was out of the burning house and safe. The firefighters worked on through the night.

The next day, traffic picked up on Warren Avenue. The

ruined house, which was now about half a shell, quickly became a minor tourist attraction. The smell of smoke still lingered in the air around the rubble.

"They ought to bulldoze the rest of it," my neighbor commented as we studied the remains from the street.

For the next few days, the sightseers kept up their pace. Then things calmed down. The burned-out shell stood lonely and abandoned as people passed on their way to work, school, and play.

One afternoon as I returned from work, the summer sounds of kids yelling, dogs barking, and lawnmowers humming were joined by another group of sounds. The buzzing of saws and the pounding of nails rang out loud and clear. The burned-out house across the street was suddenly a beehive of activity. Ladders, lumber, shingles-everything needed to rebuild down to the paint and paintbrushes was being unloaded.

Over the next several weeks, an amazing transformation took place. The burned-out shell of a house, considered by many a total loss, took on a new life. Before long, the last coat of paint was applied, and as if to affirm a new beginning, flowers bloomed in the yard. The house that had risen from the ashes to become one of the best- looking in the neighborhood, once again became a tourist attraction to admirers. To me, it became something else.

After that, whenever I faced disappointment, or failure at some goal, or when I suffered a personal loss, I stepped out onto my front porch. From there I looked across the street to the house that was once rubble, but became new again. It said to me, "You can start over. You can rebuild better and stronger. As long as you have a good foundation, you can become new again. You just have to believe."

For a strong foundation and blueprints for rebuilding, look to the Master Carpenter. *Run to the Son.*

10

Mile 4

Holy Cow

*"Let us run with
patience the race that is set
before us."*
Hebrews 12:1

"May I have your attention? Quiet please. Okay, how many of you have ever drunk a glass of milk? Raise your hand. Let's see, one . . . two . . . three . . . 37 . . . 38 . . . 39 . . . 103 . . . 104 . . . 105. Okay, great-almost everyone. You can put your hands down now. Thank you."

Several years ago a good friend of mine told me about a painting she gave to a young couple as a wedding gift. The picture was of a cow grazing in a pasture. Underneath the picture was this caption: *Patience, the grass will become milk someday.*

According to the book *American Averages* by Mike Feinsilber and William B. Mead, "On an average day in America, 10,930,000 cows are milked." So let's talk about patience and that glass of moo juice you drank today.

Do you see that cow over there eating grass? It's a dairy cow and she eats about fifty pounds of food and she drinks about fifteen gallons of water a day. Cows are able to make milk when they are two years old and have given birth to a calf. After the babies are taken away, we humans make use of the plentiful supply of milk.

I think you'll find this next bit of information *udderly* fascinating. The food eaten by a dairy cow is tough and coarse.

It's hard to digest. The cow has a special stomach to deal with this problem. Her stomach has four parts. Moo!

When the cow eats, she chews just enough to swallow her food. The food goes to the first two stomachs, which are called the rumen and the reticulum. When the cow is full she's ready for a rest.

When break time is over the cow coughs up balls of food called cud. The cow chews the cud thoroughly and then swallows it again. On this trip, the food goes to the third and fourth stomachs, which are called the omasum and the abomasum. This is where it is finally digested. Some of the food goes into the cow's bloodstream, then enters the udder where the milk is made.

Moo-ving right along.

When the udder is full, it's time to milk the cow. This is done by hand or by machine twice a day. The average cow makes five gallons of milk a day.

Next stop is the dairy, where the milk is tested, pasteurized, homogenized, packaged, and made ready for shipment to stores. Don't forget to pick up a gallon on your way home tonight.

Take a tip from the cow. When cooking up success, notice that the recipe calls for plenty of patience sifted through setbacks, disappointments, and heartaches.

The Bible says it this way: "And let us not be weary in well-doing for in due season we shall reap, if we faint not." Galatians 6:9.

Run to the Son? Yes! Run with patience? Yes! Will you get there? Yes! GUARANTEED!

14

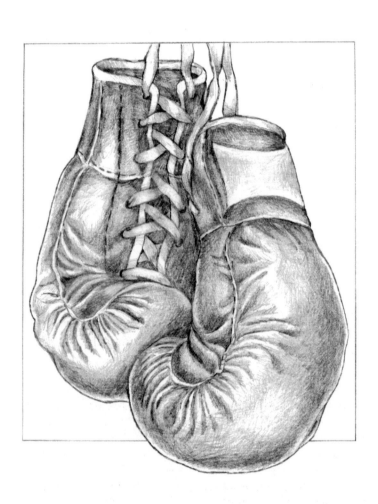

Mile 5
The Champ

*"Make your prayer
to Him and He will hear you."*
Job 22:27

On August 4, 1974, traveling by automobile my wife and I left Columbus, Ohio. My destination was Deer Lake, Pennsylvania. Just twenty miles north of Reading, Deer Lake was the location of the training camp for Muhammad Ali, heavyweight boxer and, at that time, former champion.

Just a few weeks earlier, during a television interview, Ali had invited all his fans to come up to Deer Lake and watch him train for his next fight. I decided to accept his invitation.

Arriving at the camp early Monday morning, I felt like I'd been knocked out when a member of his entourage told me the former champ was in Columbus, Ohio. I had left Columbus to go to Deer Lake at the same time he left Deer Lake to go to Columbus on business! He was scheduled to return the next day.

Before sunrise the next day, I was back at the camp. The timing was perfect. Ali was just completing a six-mile training run. I was the first fan to greet him that day. We shook hands and I introduced myself. I told him I was from Columbus and we laughed about passing each other on the highway two days before. This Ali was turning out to be a different kind of man than the one I was used to seeing on TV.

During interviews and pre-fight ballyhoos he was wild, loud, and crazy. In person, he spoke barely above a whisper.

He was polite. Our conversations centered around his upcoming fight with George Foreman, a man all the sports writers were calling invincible.

A boxing fan's dream came true when Ali said he had business in Philadelphia that day and my wife and I were welcome to travel with him. The kindness didn't stop there, either. Upon returning home, I was quick to write him a thank-you letter. In it I enclosed three pictures of him that were taken at his camp that day. He autographed them and returned them to me with this letter:

> Dear Jerry,
> I was delighted to hear from you. You may not think so, but I really appreciate each and every letter that I receive. I feel good now.
> I'm in good shape and razor sharp. In case you were a little apprehensive regarding my upcoming fight, let me inform you that this is going to be the prettiest most masterful upset that boxing has ever seen. I guarantee this, and I couldn't be more serious. Please forgive the brevity of this letter, but I have much to do and must move on. I hope you achieve success in whatever you try to do.
>
> Very truly yours,
> Muhammad Ali

In case you're not a boxing fan, the fight turned out just the way he predicted. Ali knocked out Foreman in the eighth round and was once again champion.

Here was a man who, at the time, was perhaps the most famous personality in the boxing world and beyond. Celebrities and heads of state sought out his company. For himself and others he earned millions. With all his accomplishments and accolades, he did his best to remain approachable. I was privileged to meet him.

18

What an even greater privilege it is to know someone who is and has always been even more approachable. He offers twenty-four-hour access. He has no secretary to screen his messages. No appointment is required. There is no waiting in line and no charge for his services. His name is Jesus and he is only a prayer away.

Don't run from your hurts, heartaches, and problems. Instead, *run to the Son.*

Mile 6
Fandango

Do you like riddles?

Okay, here's one for you. What do Liquid Plumber, Lee Fingernails, a Daisy toaster oven, and an Omni Chord musical instrument have in common? I'll give you a minute.

Tick . . . tock . . . tick . . . tock . . .

That's a minute. Do you give up?

The answer is Liquid Plumber, Lee Fingernails, A Daisy toaster oven, and an Omni Chord are all prizes I won on the TV game show, *Fandango*. Bet you're impressed!

Wait a second. What do you mean, you never heard of *Fandango?* Come on, now-*Fandango* is a country music trivia game show on the Nashville network.

It all started back in the spring of 1986. The marquee at Westland Shopping Center read *AUDITION FOR FANDANGO TV SHOW.* The first hurdle on the road to television stardom was a twenty-five question quiz about country music. Possible contestants have only about ten minutes to complete it. I got enough answers right for them to take my picture and say they would call me in September to come to Nashville and be on the show.

I don't have the best set of ears, but I did hear opportunity knocking. I beat feet to the library and bookstore. I read everything I could find on the history and current state of country music. I was ready.

September arrived. October arrived. November arrived. Did they forget about me?

December arrived. January arrived. February arrived. I was sure they forgot about me.

March arrived. They called. They hadn't forgotten about me! "Come to Nashville," they said. Yee-haw! I was on my way.

When I arrived, they weren't as ready to hang a star on my dressing room door as I thought they would be. Another audition was required, this time in front of the show's producer. There would be lights and cameras, just like the real thing. The plan was to tape five shows that day. The contestants showing the greatest poise, fastest response, and most enthusiasm during auditions would be picked for the real McCoy. I was selected for the second show to be taped that day.

Lights, camera, action . . . here we go. Now listen to the question. Be the first one to ring the buzzer . . . You got it. Merle Haggard is the right answer. Ten points for you and on to the next question . . . and so it went.

We got down to the last few minutes of the game. I was a few points behind, but if I got the next question right and my remaining opponent got it wrong, I would be the winner. Then I would have the opportunity to receive the major prizes in the next round of competition.

In my imagination, I was already driving the new car and sailing the new boat I was going to win. The show's host, Bill Anderson, presented the final question: "What year did Jimmy Dean have a hit with the recording of *Big Bad John?*"

Here's a hint. It was the same year the United States sent its first astronaut into outer space. What do you say?

I said 1962 and that was wrong. The correct answer is 1961.

Yes, I blew it-it was all over. Fortunately for you and

me, life is not a TV game show and we never have to worry about disqualification.

Remember, no matter the question, the correct answer is Jesus. *Keep running to the Son.*

Mile 7
Sign My Book, Please

> *"If you have faith
> as a mustard seed, you will
> say to this mountain, 'Move
> from here to there', and it
> will move; and nothing will
> be impossible for you."*
> Matthew 17:20

One of my all-time favorite comedians is Henny Youngman. Henny was known as the king of one-liners because he never delivered a joke that took more than twenty-four seconds to tell. His most famous one-liner was "Take my wife-please." Thanks to the wonder of video and audio recordings the late Henny Youngman is still enjoying the spotlight as a performer.

A short time before his death, after reading his autobiography, I called him in New York. I complimented him on the book and his long, successful career of making people laugh. Next, I asked if I could send him a copy of the book and requested the honor of his autograph. In less than a week, he returned the book with this inscription:

Hello Jerry, have someone read this to you.
Henny Youngman (Himself)

I love to read. Several years ago, while Christmas shopping in a bookstore, I saw a sign that offered this advice: Give someone a book. It's the gift they can open more than once.

For me, that's true and it always adds a special dimension to my reading when I'm able to obtain an autograph and sometimes a handshake from the author.

My collection of autographed books include volumes by ministers Norman Vincent Peale, Robert Schuller, Davey Roever, teacher Sam Keen, entrepreneur Dave Thomas, runner Harry (Hal) Lewis, former Marine Corp Lt. Colonel Oliver North, and baseball great Dave Dravecky.

Motivational speaker/writer Carl Mays autographed his book, *A Strategy for Winning* this way:

> *To Jerry,*
> *Those who can see the invisible can do the impossible.*
> *Carl Mays 11/19/91*

One of the most delightful people I have ever had the privilege of meeting is Mamie McCullough. She wrote a book called, *I Can, You Can Too!* and she signed it to me with a reference to Philippians 4:13: "I can do all things through Christ who strengthens me."

Mamie was born into financial poverty along with eight brothers and sisters. She was a sexually abused child. Her mother became a widow just four years after Mamie was born. With more heartaches following her along the way, you might say she had more than enough reason to walk through life carrying a chip on her shoulder.

"A chip on your shoulder is a sign of wood up above," I heard her tell an audience.

With hard work and diligent study, she graduated from college, became a teacher, businesswoman, writer, and inspirational speaker. Instead of a chip, Mamie chooses to wear on her shoulder a decorative pin in the likeness of a bee.

Why a bee?

26

Aerodynamically speaking, the bumble bee is not supposed to be able to fly. Its body is too big-its wings too small. The bee flies anyway. No one bothered to tell the bee it wasn't supposed to fly or, if they did tell the bee it couldn't fly, then the bee didn't listen. It flies, simply because it *bee-lieves* that it can.

The *run to the Son* starts with bee-lieving.

Laughter Wins Howard's Hill

*"A merry heart doeth
good like medicine."*
Proverbs 17:22

Where were you in the summer of 1970? I was in boot camp at the Marine Corps Recruit Depot in San Diego, California. While receiving instructions at the rifle range, I heard another recruit being asked what would happen if one of his ears was shot off. The recruit replied that he wouldn't be able to hear.

"And what if you get both ears shot off, then what?"

"I wouldn't be able to see," replied the recruit.

"What do you mean, you wouldn't be able to see?" the angry drill instructor shouted as he grabbed the recruit by the collar.

"You see, sir," the recruit explained. "If I got both ears shot off, then my helmet would slide down over my eyes and I wouldn't be able to see."

I spent two years, eleven months, and twenty-three days in the marines. Sadly, I never met John Wayne, Bob Hope, or Gomer Pyle. Fortunately, though, I never had to serve in combat. In fact, I might have done just as well to join the navy, since I spent most of my service time as part of the marine detachment aboard the USS *Oriskany*, an aircraft carrier.

The ship cruised off the coast of Vietnam, while its airplanes flew bombing missions. The Gulf of Tonkin was as close as I got to Vietnam. While I drew combat pay each month and enjoyed the safety of the ship, many marines were not so fortunate. For example, Staff Sergeant Jimmie Howard and seventeen other marines who found themselves on Hill 488 in Vietnam. They were a reconnaissance platoon stationed there in order to direct air and artillery strikes against enemy supply lines.

The North Vietnamese had committed several hundred troops to the task of destroying the marines. The battle raged through the night. When they ran out of hand grenades, Sergeant Howard directed his men to throw rocks. They did. When the North Vietnamese started a predawn chant, "Hey, marines, you die in one hour," Sergeant Howard directed his men to laugh-and they did. They laughed as loudly and as hysterically as they could.

The North Vietnamese soldiers must have concluded there were more than a few marines on Hill 488 and whatever the number, they had to be crazy to be laughing at certain death. The attack, which would have certainly annihilated Sergeant Howard and his men, never happened.

Help arrived the next day and the marines on Howard's Hill, as it became known, had psyched out the enemy with laughter. They became one of the most decorated platoons in history: eighteen Purple Hearts, thirteen Silver Stars, four Navy Crosses and, for Sergeant Jimmie Howard, the Medal of Honor.

In our day-to-day living, few of us ever face such adverse situations as Sergeant Howard and his men did on that hill in Vietnam. But, life being what it is, we do find ourselves up against difficult and challenging circumstances. Many times the outcome will not be clear to us. At this point, our options are few. Choose the path of laughter and *keep running to the Son.* It just might save your life-ask Sergeant Howard.

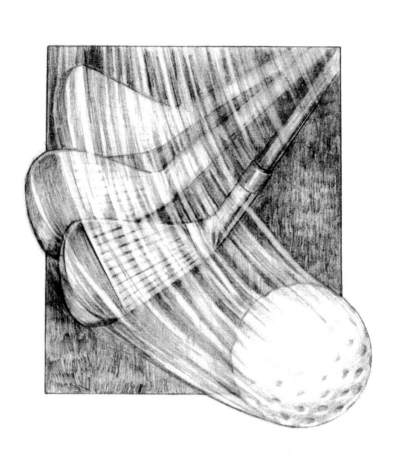

Look Out, No, I Mean . . . Fore!

> *"For as he thinks in his heart so is he."*
> Proverbs 23:7

Does fresh air, exercise, and easy money sound appealing to you? It did to me when I was in elementary and junior high school. I especially liked the part about easy money. That's why I got a job as a caddie at the local golf course. I carried clubs for all kinds of characters, some nice and some not so nice. I heard them tell lots of golf stories and jokes. I suspect this joke was around long before I was and will be around long after I'm gone:

"Why does the crazy golfer wear two pairs of pants when he plays?"

Do you give up?

"He wears two pairs of pants in case he gets a hole in one."

Think about it.

Now wait, before you boo me off the stage, let me ask you something. Who is your favorite golfer? Is it Jack Nicklaus, Lee Trevino? Nancy Lopez, Babe Zaharias, Arnold Palmer, Chi Chi Rodriguez or perhaps Tiger Woods? How about Lieutenant Colonel George Hall?

You've never heard of Lieutenant Colonel George Hall? Maybe not. You won't find his name in any record books next to the names of the other golfers I mentioned. In fact, you may not find his name in any book dealing with the topic of golf. But still, he's the golfer I admire most. Let me tell you why.

Lieutenant Colonel George Hall was an air force combat pilot flying missions over North Vietnam when his plane was shot out from under him. He parachuted to safety but was quickly taken prisoner. Before this unfortunate twist of fate, he had been an avid golfer. His score averaged in the mid seventies. He would not hold a real golf club in his hands or see a real golf course for the next seven years. He spent five and a half of those years as a prisoner of war in solitary confinement. Locked up in an eight-foot by eight-foot cell, all alone for five and a half years, what would you do?

Colonel Hall played golf. How? In his imagination.

Every day for those long years in confinement, Colonel Hall played eighteen holes of golf. In his mind he reviewed every aspect of the game. How to set up a shot, hold a club, the proper stance, the correct swing, the chip, the putt . . . anything related to the game of golf ran like a movie in his imagination over and over again. When he ran out of things to remember about old golf courses he had played on, then his imagination designed, built, and played on new ones.

In 1973 the war ended and Colonel Hall came home. The years of enduring that living hell had weakened all but his spirit. Two weeks later, he played in a golf tournament. This time, the clubs and the course were real.

How did he do? He shot a seventy-six. Was it luck?

"No," he said. "Are you kidding? I never three-putted a green in all my five-and-a-half years of practice."

On your journey through life there will be roadblocks, detours and surprises. Look inside yourself. Imagine victory. It's waiting for you. *Just keep running to the Son.*

Mile 10
Boston, New York . . .?

*"For God so loved the
world that he gave his only
begotten son, that whosoever
believeth in him should not
perish, but have everlasting life."*
John 3:16

No and no. These are my answers to the two questions
that will eventually surface in any conversation among marathon runners. Have you ever run in the Boston Marathon? Have
you ever run in the New York Marathon?

These are probably the two best known marathon races.
Whether you're a runner or not, chances are you've heard of
them. So, your next question for me is no doubt going to be,
"Why haven't you run in these races?"

For Boston, you must qualify to run by completing another marathon in a prescribed time for your age category. So
far, I haven't made the qualifying time (but keep reading, I may
by the end of this book). For New York, where there are around
20,000 runners, you're selected by entering a lottery or you can
win a contest, as I tried to do in 1992.

Runner's World magazine advertised a contest with top
prize being an all expense paid trip to New York and guaranteed
entry in the *marathon* race. All you had to do was "Come up
with new and innovative uses of the word marathon," they said.

After coming up with 300 ideas, I narrowed it down to
twenty six, the maximum number of entries for the contest, and
mailed them in. Here they are:

- *Eat Marathon Bananas* / They're long on appeal.
- *Marathon of Love* / What you call an all-day tennis match with no score.
- *Join the Marathon Parachute Club* / We have miles of openings for new members.
- *Send Marathon Greeting Cards* / When there's miles between your smiles.
- *Join the Marathon Church* / Find a beginning with no end.
- *Marathon Auto Bumpers* / It's okay to keep running into us.
- *Marathon Kiss* / What you call a career at the Hershey's Chocolate Factory.
- *Marathon Glue* / Going the extra mile to stick it to 'em.
- *Marathon House Paint* / It won't run.
- *Marathon Dentistry* / We'll keep you running from one smile to the next.
- *Marathon Dry Cleaners* / We never run out of steam.
- *Marathon Tools* / We'll outlast the work to be done.
- *Marathon Cold Relief Medicine* / When you want your feet to do the running instead of your nose.
- *Marathon Computers* / Our chips are never down.
- *Marathon Rice* / The long grain.
- *Marathon Toothpaste & Mouthwash* / It keeps working, smile after smile.
- *Marathon Pickles* / Miles of thrills with our dills.
- *Marathon Clocks & Watches* / We never run out of time.
- *Marathon Reading Festival* / At the library . . . etc . . . etc . . . etc.
- *Marathon Dog Waste Removal* / As long as they're poopin', we're scoopin.

38

- *Marathon Burgers* / So big you'll think you ordered two.
- *Marathon Car Wash* / For a lasting shine to your finish.
- *Marathon Smile* / What you'll have tomorrow if you sleep with a coat hanger in your mouth tonight.
  - *Choose Marathon Rocking Chairs* / When you want to get nowhere all day long.
  - Are you feeling risqué'? Then *Eat at the Marathon Fish Market* / We never run out of cheap gills.
  - *Wear Marathon Pantyhose* / You keep running-they won't.

If you're like me, then you're next question is, why didn't I win? For some reason that, to this day, eludes me, the judges picked another contestant.

Take another look at John 3:16. *Everlasting Life*, now that's a marathon. The really great thing about this verse is that it doesn't mention a qualifying time, a lottery, or a contest. The only requirement for the *Run to the Son* is believing.

Hope I see you at the finish line.

39

Mile II
Camp Chase

"You shall know the
truth, and the truth shall
make you free."
John 8:32

Joseph Abbott, John Barber, James Beckett, Frank Bigsby, John Calvin, Charles Coy, George Davis, Joel Dillion, Charles Green, Thomas Hall, Curtis Hook . . .

If I were to continue this list, I would have to add another 2,249 names. These are the names of confederate soldiers who were laid to rest at Camp Chase Cemetery in Columbus, Ohio. It's the largest confederate cemetery in the north. These Civil War soldiers died while being held prisoner at the camp. The cemetery is all that remains of the once bustling camp. First built to organize and train recruits to fight the rebels, it soon swelled to capacity with prisoners from the south.

Houses, a church, a library, a gas station, and other assorted modern buildings now occupy the space where once soldiers sat in crude, wooden barracks and dreamed of home. For 2,260 young men, the dream never came true. Harsh winters, deplorable sanitary conditions and all the accompanying misfortunes of war stole their future.

A Civil War reenactment camp has been staged on a baseball field near the cemetery during recent summers. There, you can experience firsthand the way Civil War soldiers from both sides lived, marched, cooked, camped, and fought.

Several groups and organizations have representatives

there who will offer you tips on tracing your Civil War genealogy. Now you can find out what distant cousins and great-great grandfathers contributed to this chapter of American history. You'll know who fought on what side, in what battles, and what happened to them.

Reenactment units, people who pretend to be Civil War soldiers, are more than enthusiastic to share their knowledge about equipment and tactics. If you're interested, they will take you on as a new recruit. Vendors are set up to sell you all the clothes, badges, buttons, shoes, guns, and other equipment to create your Civil War uniform. Not to be outdone by the men, there are plenty of costumes for the ladies who wish to dress 1860s style. To round it all out, there are stacks of books on the subject of the Civil War to entertain and educate you long after the reenactment camp has broken and all the players return to modern life.

Two days later, the field transforms from a Civil War camp back to a baseball field. Once again, all that remains of Camp Chase is the cemetery.

Chances are you've never heard of the place until now. In most conversations about the Civil War, Camp Chase isn't mentioned in the same sentence with names like Gettysburg, Antietam, Bull Run, and Fort Sumter.

These are important places, and what happened there should not be forgotten, but if history is our teacher, then there is a lesson to be learned from Camp Chase. We're a lot like those soldiers buried there. We are all held prisoner, confined by anger, hate, jealousy, and greed. The good news is we don't have to wait for a surrender to be signed and cell doors to be unlocked.

Run to the Son and His truth shall make you free.

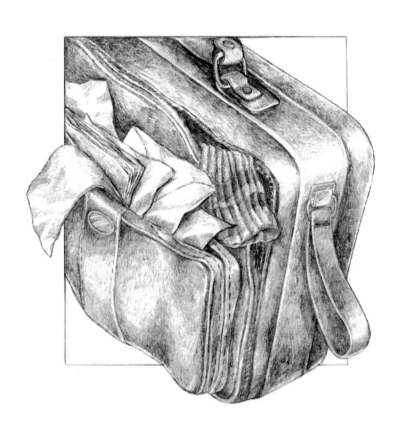

What's In Your Suitcase?

*"This is the day the
Lord has made; we will rejoice
and be glad in it."*
Psalm 118:24

"Hey, that smells good! What are you cooking? I can't wait to taste it."

I've never heard those words directed at me. In fact, if the response to my cooking is any indication, then Betty Crocker and Sara Lee have nothing to worry about. Their jobs are secure. After six weeks in a cooking class at Ohio State University, my only crowning achievement was to walk away knowing I could bake a batch of date nut bars.

"Care to try one? No? Okay, maybe later."

Even though, for reasons I haven't figured out yet, I didn't learn how to cook like Betty and Sara, I did enjoy the class. While exploring the pages of a cookbook, I ran across some quotations. I guess you would call them food for thought. My favorite was this:

"Our days are identical suitcases, all the same size, but some people pack more into them than others."

There was no indication in the book whom to attribute the quote to or what kind of cook they turned out to be. So, while enjoying my next meal in a restaurant, I began to ponder what was in my suitcase.

Before deciding, I took another look at the quote. "Our days are identical suitcases . . ." it began. It made no mention of how many days (suitcases) we will have. No guarantees. No one knows when they're packing and unpacking for the last time. If I were taking a vacation, I said to myself, and could only take one suitcase instead of twenty, I know I would spend considerable time figuring out what to take and what to leave behind.

Dreams, goals, time with friends and family-those are in there right beside clean underwear and a toothbrush. When it comes to words, I hope my suitcase holds plenty of thank yous, pleases and, most importantly, I love yous. A sense of humor is essential no matter what kind of traveling you're doing. I put it next to forgiveness. After looking at the quote again, I realized there are some items in my suitcase that I really don't need. They are worry, resentment, anger, and guilt.

At this point, I should have been ready to close the lid and get on with the rest of the day, but something inside me wouldn't let it rest. I decided to take a survey among friends, family and co-workers. I handed out twenty-five questionnaires with the quote and asked people to tell me what it meant to them, what was in their suitcase, and what was missing.

Five people didn't have the time in their suitcase to answer. Twenty-four hours didn't seem long enough, but that is all the time we get in a day. Of the twenty who did respond, most had trouble getting the lid shut and *fun* was the first item to be tossed out.

Work, school, and other obligations certainly have their place. I vote for a little less anxiety and a little more joy. Come on, folks, not all the news is bad. It's not a round trip ticket we've been given. What's in your suitcase? Smell the roses and *keep running to the Son.*

46

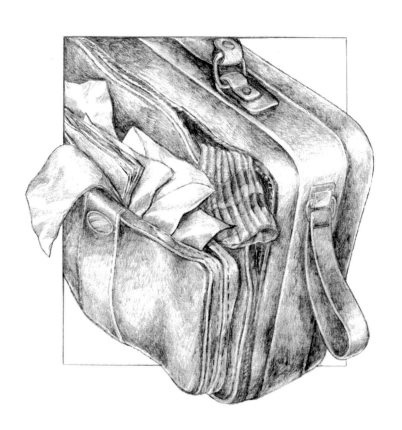

Mile 13

Dear Santa

*"Giving thanks
always, for all things, to
God the Father in the name
of our Lord Jesus Christ."*
Ephesians 5:20

I didn't want to be in school, much less at a Christmas assembly in the auditorium. I can't tell you what songs were sung that day, how the place was decorated, or who sat next to whom. When my memory replays good times, I'm afraid junior high school rarely gets a flicker. However, I often remember part of a speech from that day. Now, almost three decades later, it still humbles me.

Like everything else concerning school, I was trying to tune out the speech. I managed to forget the speaker's name right away, if I even heard it. What he looked like and what he was wearing-that's gone too. I don't know how long he spoke, if he got polite applause, or a standing ovation.

In spite of all my efforts not to hear what that speaker had to say, he told a story that penetrated my brain that day and has stayed there ever since. When I'm feeling ungrateful, the story bumps its way out of storage and runs across my mind like a movie.

The man at the assembly that day was relating in great detail his experience as a postal worker at Christmas time. One of the rights of passage for most children is to write a letter to Santa Claus and, although I've never delivered mail, I suppose second only to being attacked by a hungry dog, the extra load of cards, letters, and packages at Christmas time leads most postal workers to consider another line of work.

Part of the speaker's job was dealing with hundreds of letters addressed to Santa Claus. All the letters were received well before Christmas Eve, giving Santa plenty of time to act on the requests for the latest and hottest toys, dolls, bikes, sports equipment, and clothes. The letter writers went to great lengths in explaining their requests, with careful detail as to size shape, color, and quantity. If Santa made good on all these deliveries, he would deserve a long vacation.

Christmas came and Christmas went. The new year was only hours away, but what did the mail worker find in the next bag of mail to be sorted? One more letter addressed to Santa.

"This one is a little late," the worker mumbled as he tossed it aside and tried to get on with his work, but he kept thinking about that letter. In fact, he couldn't seem to get it out of his mind. Finally, curiosity prodded him to sit down, tear open and read the letter.

Tears quickly clouded his vision. It wasn't the standard "Dear Santa" followed by a list of I want this and I want that. No, this letter was different from any other Dear Santa letter.

> *Dear Santa,*
> *Thank you for coming to my house.*
> *Thank you for the nice clothes.*
> *Thank you for the new bike.*
> *Thank you for the ice skates.*
> *Thank you for the nice presents you brought to my brother and sister even though they weren't good all the time.*
> *Thank you for eating the cookies I made for you and for washing out the cup after you drank the hot chocolate.*
> *Thank you for being so nice to me even though*

50

*Dad got mad last week and said you probably wouldn't
bring me anything.*
Thank you for a happy Christmas!
Thank you for reading my letter.

See you next year,
Love Casey

I plead guilty. Too often I treat God the way those kids
treated Santa. Hundreds of "I wants" and far too few "Thank
yous."

Run with the attitude of gratitude and *Run to the Son.*

51

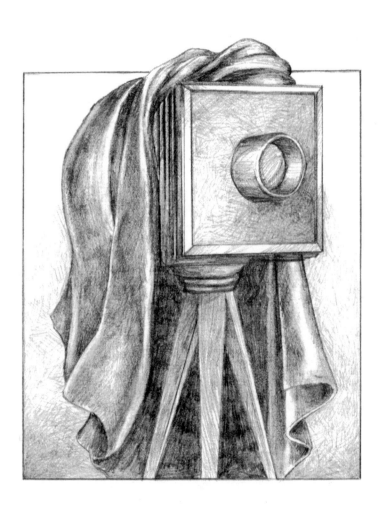

Mile 14
Say Cheese

*"And we know that
all things work together for
good to them that love
God, to them who are
called according to his
purpose."*
Romans 8:28

"Ready, please. Stand up straight and move just a little to the right. Perfect. *Say cheese.* Got it. Let me take one more so I can finish this roll . . ."

Speaking of picture taking and pictures, here's another quote we have to credit to *Anonymous.* "Character is like camera film, both are developed in the dark."

Several years ago, during an informal conversation, I asked a professional photographer if there were any famous people included in his portfolio. He had some politicians and small town celebrities but without a doubt, the most famous and perhaps the most important picture in his personal collection was not one that he took. It was one he discovered.

During World War I, an American doughboy looking for souvenirs took possession of a camera belonging to a captured German soldier. The year was 1918. When the war ended, the American returned home to celebrate victory and become a civilian again. The camera he brought with him was put on a closet shelf. It remained in storage for nearly forty years.

When photographer John Millirons was given the camera as a gift, he discovered it still contained film. All those years the camera had rested in a cool dry place. Was it possible that the film was still in good condition?

In the darkroom, the mystery locked inside the camera began to unfold. As the pictures were developed, they gave testimony to the quality of the camera, its film, and the brutality of war. Among the gruesome scenes of the battlefield, one picture stood out from the others. It showed an American airplane lying in rubble on the ground. There were identification marks clearly visible on a section of the wreckage. On the ground beside the airplane lay the dead pilot. His fatal wounds were evident.

Copies of the pictures were sent to the Air Force Museum in Washington. From the marking on the downed American aircraft and the view of its pilot, his identity was confirmed. First Lt. Quentin Roosevelt was the pilot. Up to that moment, Teddy Roosevelt's son had been listed as missing in action. The secret of this warrior's fate had been locked in that camera for nearly four decades.

Ponder this theory. Our lives are often like that camera film. Something negative happens, like a setback in reaching a goal or difficulty in a relationship. Speaking from experience, I'm often reluctant or just plain afraid to deal with the matter. Sometimes, the truth waiting to come to light is not a pleasant one, as in the fate of Quentin Roosevelt, but if we are to grow spiritually and emotionally, we have to face the truth and prepare to move on.

When the negatives of your life threaten to break you, don't be afraid to take them into the darkroom. Develop them there into something beautiful with the help of the master photographer. *Run to the Son.*

54

Mile 15
A Really Big Show

*"Be of good
courage and He shall
strengthen your heart, all
ye that hope in the Lord."*
Psalms 31:23

Twenty-two years after graduation, at age forty, I had pretty much given up on the idea of being in a high school play, but as the great Winston Churchill said, "Never, never, never, never give up!"

So I didn't. When my daughter was cast in her school's production of *Bye Bye Birdie*, I remarked to some of her friends that I'd like to play the part of Ed Sullivan. After all, I'd been preparing for the role most of my life.

I grew up watching Ed Sullivan. If you were looking for me on Sunday night, chances are pretty good you would find me in front of the TV watching his show. Dancers, puppets, mimes, bears, horses, dogs, jugglers, comics, actors, and sports heroes- Ed Sullivan had them all. Any performer knew they had *made it* if they landed a guest appearance on his show.

What was the secret of his appeal? Most pundits of TV agree. Ed Sullivan made it look like anyone could do his job.

He often made mistakes, fumbled names, and tripped over announcements. He was a happy man, but had a stiff cardboard appearance that made him look like he was wearing his jacket with the coat hanger still in it. He was an entertainer everyone could enjoy and his show was safe for the whole family. A lot of people made an attempt at imitating him. Some professionals even made a living at it. Although I was never paid for it, I got pretty good at being Ed Sullivan.

"Now, right here on our stage . . . a really big shoe!" (Show always sounded like shoe when Ed said it.)

The Upper Arlington High School production of *Bye Bye Birdie* went into rehearsal without me. I went back to minding my own business and occasionally acted like Ed for my own amusement.

As a wise old sage once said, "Be careful what you ask for. You might get it." I wouldn't say they were desperate, but opening night was only a week away and they still hadn't cast the role of Ed Sullivan. The kids didn't forget me. They told their director about my aspirations. A short time later, opportunity dialed my phone number and I was on my way.

The play called for Ed to deliver a few short lines of introduction. This would take place off stage, while some scenery was moved about. In other words, the audience would never see Ed, only hear him.

The director recited over the phone what lines were required and I copied them down. Next, I moved into the recording studio. To the average pair of eyes, it may have looked like a cheap tape recorder in a bathroom, but to me, it was Broadway.

After a few rehearsals, I cued up the record button. A couple of nights later, by way of tape recorder, I was performing in the play.

Now, let me borrow a line from Robert Schuller: "God's delays are not God's denials."

Choose courage and hope as your partners and *keep running to the Son.*

58

Mile 16
Sherman

*"Not that I speak in
regard to need for I have
learned in whatever state I
am, to be content."*
Philippians 4:11

I like history. Like a great many people these days, I'm fascinated with the American Civil War. Recently I did a little genealogical work. I shook the family tree and plenty of relatives who fought in the Civil War fell out. It looked like an even match concerning loyalty. Typical of those times, my family filled the ranks of both the blue and the gray.

For example, Benjamin Washington Beery built the iron-clad ship *North Carolina* and steamer *Yadkin* for the confederate government. Another distant cousin, Isaac Newton Beery, rode in the confederate cavalry under the command of General "Jeb" Stuart. Peter Beery believed slavery was wrong. The confederates tried to draft him in the winter of 1862. With two other men, he abandoned all his possessions, escaped from Virginia, and made his way to safety in Ohio. Jacob Wenger, a peace advocate, was not so lucky. He was forced to serve in the confederate army.

On the Yankee side, Joseph C. Beery died in the gruesome rebel prison at Andersonville. Richard T. Berkly died fighting to save the Union. John H. Hufford became disabled in the war. George Mericle, Aaron Neft, George W. Sheets, and Benoni

Beery were all branches of the family tree that marched for the northern cause.

One of the most colorful and famous characters of the Civil War was General William Tecumseh Sherman. Two of my relatives served with him. Henry Samuel Beery, of the 114th Regular Ohio Volunteer Infantry, fought under Sherman's command at such places as Chicksaw Bayou, Fort Hindman, Port Gibson, Thompson's Hill, Champion Hills, Big Black River Bridge and the siege of Vicksburg. Daniel M. Beery lied about his age in order to enlist in the army. He was with Sherman during the famous *March to the Sea.*

About thirty minutes southeast of where I live in Columbus, Ohio, is the town of Lancaster. This is the birthplace of General Sherman. His childhood home has been transformed into a museum. For only two dollars, you can tour the house built in 1811. It has been restored so you can see much of it the way young William Sherman and his siblings viewed it. In addition to family memorabilia, there is also a room containing a recreation of General Sherman's field tent, some of the general's personal gear, and other Civil War exhibits. The Sherman House is a must-see for all history scholars.

Of course, when studying General Sherman, the focus is usually on his contributions to winning the Civil War. That's great and certainly important, but there is another story about Sherman in which I find comfort and hope.

Sherman had red hair, and at a young age he hated it. In fact, he hated it so much that he tried to dye it another color. He was successful-unfortunately his victory was a hollow one since the resultant color was green. Later, when his hair had grown back to red, someone convinced him that Indians like to scalp redheaded boys, and he took a different view. His red hair became a symbol of courage and defiance. Same hair, different attitude.

Some things can't be changed, but by *running to the Son* our attitude about them can.

Mile 17

Repeat Offender

*"For if ye forgive
men their trespasses your
heavenly father will also
forgive you."*
Matthew 6:14

I've just cashed a check from a bank in Hollywood, California, but the envelope it came in was postmarked Mansfield, Ohio. It's not the first time something like this has happened. Like most states, Ohio has to keep building new prisons to accommodate the people we hear about every night on the news. That leaves some older structures empty.

In the past fourteen years, I've been sent to prison three times. No, I didn't rob a bank, steal a car, sell drugs, or commit murder. Many of the old, empty prisons have been used as movie sets and I've worked those sets as an extra.

Who said, "Crime doesn't pay?" I received minimum wage, lunch, and an opportunity to be discovered. That's what Hollywood had to offer when they wheeled into town with truckloads of cameras, lights, and costumes. So far, I've eaten the free lunch and spent the money. I'm still waiting to be discovered.

As a movie extra or, as we're sometimes called, *atmosphere artists*, my job was to work in the background and make stars like Robert Redford and Morgan Freeman look good. In the films *Brubaker*, *Attica*, and *The Shawshank Redemption*, I received a short haircut, rumpled prison uniform and, sometimes, an application of make-up to make me look like a hard-hearted convict capable of the most grisly crimes imaginable.

In spite of my brilliant talents for digging graves, loading lumber, throwing debris, and shouting profanities on the screen, the Academy Awards representatives have mysteriously overlooked my name. How do you suppose that happened?

Although I never received a chair with my name on the back or a limo ride to the set each morning, for the most part I was treated well by the movie crews. It wasn't hard work. A lot of time and thinking goes into setting up a shot, lighting the set, planning camera angles, and preparing props. That leaves plenty of down time for the extras.

"Quiet on the set. We're rolling. Camera . . . action . . . cut . . . back to one . . ." and so it goes. We keep repeating it until the director is satisfied with the scene. "Cut . . . that's a print. Now get ready for the next scene. Extras, fill in over here. Remember, you're hot, you're hungry, you're tired, and you're mean. Make it look real."

At this point, those of us with stars in our eyes maneuver for a good camera angle. That way, friends, family, and talent scouts will see us on the big screen. Finally, the director shouts, "That's a wrap!" After trading prison clothes for my own, I am free to walk out the gate.

"See you tomorrow!"

Three movies and three times a prisoner. I just can't make it out of jail. As far as Hollywood is concerned, I'm a repeat offender.

In real life, I also make mistakes. You do the same. Let's forgive each other, and together, *run to the Son*, seeking his forgiveness.

Mile 18
Twice as Smart

*"Being confident
of this very thing, that he
who has begun a good
work in you will complete it."*
Philippians 1:6

After ducking out a rear door and running down a street where I was sure no other kids would be, I let my eyes explode in tears. Actually, I couldn't stop them from exploding. I had just flunked fourth grade. Devastated, feeling worthless, I pushed on, knowing I was branded "stupid" for life.

I didn't know one set of eyes could cry that many tears. When my alternate route failed me as an escape and the neighbor's kids saw me, it got worse. I'm sure that arrows would have hurt less than the words from those kids. It didn't feel like my most shining moment. All these years later, I realize-maybe it was.

At the top of my list of suggestions for school administrators and teachers, you'll find the word *ballbat*. At some point, most kids play baseball, watch it, collect cards with pictures of their favorite players, and drift off to sleep with dreams of playing in the major leagues.

Since they are already thinking baseball, the first time a child walks into a schoolroom, the first thing a teacher should hand him is a baseball bat. Not a big one, used to play the game, but a tiny *ballbat* carried on a key chain.

Now, along with this gift, the first lesson ought to be

about Babe Ruth. Every kid needs to know that while Babe Ruth had the record for hitting the most home runs, 714, he also held the record for the most strikeouts, 1,330. Twice as much failure as success, and yet Babe Ruth was the greatest player of his time.

After a student has carried this tiny bat through grade school, junior high, and high school, why not hang it on their graduation cap, next to their tassel? That would serve as a reminder that the game of life is just starting. Sometimes you're going to strike out. That's okay. Your turn will come again. The next swing could bring a home run.

My second suggestion concerns Abraham Lincoln. After touring the battlefield and standing in the place where Lincoln made his famous speech, I have new reverence for the Gettysburg Address. Everybody who ever went to school has heard about that speech and most had to make an attempt to memorize it. I suggest young students also learn these facts about Lincoln:

* He failed in business in 1831.
* He was defeated for the legislature in 1832.
* He failed in business again in 1833.
* After being elected to the legislature in 1834, the girl he planned to marry died.
* In 1838 he was defeated in his bid for Speaker of the House.
* He was defeated for the office of Elector in 1840 and for Congress in 1843.
* After being elected to Congress in 1846, he was defeated for that office in 1848, the Senate in 1855, vice president in 1856 and the Senate, again, in 1858.
* Finally, in 1860 he was elected President of the United States.

Babe Ruth and Abraham Lincoln, two failures and two reasons failing the fourth grade has made me *twice as smart.*

70

Failure is not rejection. It is only redirection. To find your way, *keep running to the Son.*

Mile 19
Where's the Real One?

"Wherefore take
unto you the whole armor
of God."
Ephesians 6:13

"Let me hear you say, Ho, Ho, Ho."

I complied with my friend Gary's request then, on my own, added, "Merry Christmas." I had with me a church bulletin which carried an appeal for someone to be Santa Claus in the Christmas program. The intriguing thing about the advertisement was that they wanted as many Santas as they could recruit.

"Go for it!" Gary said.

In the middle of bumping into shoppers and stringing decorations, my friend and I were sharing memories.

"You won't believe the feeling. It's almost magic when you put on a Santa suit," Gary said.

His eyes were twinkling. I could see the transformation in him as he relived the role of Santa Claus. He spared no detail in describing the process of getting into costume, that first look in the mirror, and the wonder and excitement that filled the faces of the children he met. By the time he finished talking, he had completely sold me on the idea that my next acting role had to be Jolly Ol' St. Nick.

Finding the costume was no problem and its magic began to work as soon as I took it out of the bag. For the church program, we ended up with a total of three Santas. The children were assembled on stage. They had a few lines of dialogue between the songs they were singing. One such exchange involved some kids reporting to each other where they had spotted Santa Claus that day.

"How could he be here and how could he be there at the same time?" they wondered.

While they were bouncing this question back and forth, we three Santas were passing out candy in the audience. Our backs were turned to each other until we collided in the middle of the room. At that point, we turned and jumped back in surprise as the children began singing, "Where's the real one?" It was fun-a lot of fun. Gary was right.

I highly recommend that everyone put on a Santa suit at least once in their lifetime. If there are any psychiatrists or other mental health workers reading this who are actively treating patients for depression, take note. To your list of treatments and cures, add the recommendation to dress up as Santa Claus. You can't help but feel good. If you do nothing more than look at yourself in the mirror and "Ho, ho, ho," around the house all day, it's worth the investment of your time and energy.

I also recommend that every day you dress in the whole armor of God. It's true, the same kinds of problems and heartaches will befall believers as well as nonbelievers, but with the armor described in the book of Ephesians, the believer has a whole new set of tools to deal with the challenge.

Put on your armor and *keep running to the Son.*

Mile 20
Flippo

*"For I am the Lord,
I do not change."*
Malach 3:6

Do you mind if I ask you a few questions . . .

• When was the last time you cried?

• What was your very first childhood job for money?

• What has given you pleasure during the past year?

• What does it take to make you mad?

• What is your worse phobia or fear?

• What is the most important lesson you've learned to date?

• Which of your personal character traits would you most like to change?

• If you could be someone else, who would it be and why?

• How do you face a new day?

• In one or two words, describe how you enter a crowded room.

You may be wondering if this is an application for the police force or, perhaps, the ministry. I think you'll be surprised. These questions, and more just as thought- provoking, were part of an application to Ringling Brothers and Barnum and Bailey Clown College. Yes, you heard me right, clown college.

Every year, Ringling Brothers received about 6,000 applications to attend its famous clown college located at their winter quarters in Florida. Out of the 6,000 people who applied, sixty were to be chosen to attend the school. Half of those who graduated would be offered contracts to go on the road with The Greatest Show on Earth.

During the ten weeks at clown college, an aspiring funnyperson spent long hours learning the history of circus clowning, how to apply make-up, create a character, build props, juggle, walk on stilts, ride an elephant, and create and perform comedy routines. After a thirty year existence, either Ringling decided it had cranked out enough clowns or they heard I was interested in becoming a student. Before I could get there, they closed their school.

I love the circus and I love clowns. For many years one of the local TV stations in Central Ohio featured a personality known as Flippo, King of the Clowns. He was an institution. Everyone knew him. Everyone loved him. I'll bet he could have been elected mayor.

I was still very young when the magic of Flippo came to a sad end for me. During the summer, the TV station he worked for and the Red Cross cosponsored "Learn To Swim" programs. Flippo came to visit the pool where I took lessons. The crowd of kids I was with swarmed around him. His back was to me and the giant collar he wore was slightly flipped away from its normal position. I could see where clown-white make-up ended and real people skin started. I was devastated.

What a disappointment. Flippo wasn't really Flippo all the time. He was a man dressed like a clown. How could that be? Fortunately, years later, I found someone to take Flippo's place. "Jesus Christ is the same yesterday, today and forever." Hebrews 13:8

For the real thing, *keep running to the Son.*

Mile 21
Giggles

*"A time for every
purpose . . . a time to
laugh."*
Ecclesiastes 3:4

"Thank you, thank you very much. It's a pleasure to be here. Believe me. It's not only a pleasure, it's a miracle. I just got back from Chicago and you know, that place has a reputation for being rough. I was there to run the Chicago Marathon. A marathon race is 26.2 miles and the course took us through some really tough neighborhoods. I mean, really tough. In one neighborhood several of the people I was running with had their *kneecaps stolen."*

"Actually, the rough neighborhoods helped my finish time. I always run better when I hear a siren behind me."

"It was rough, I tell you. In one neighborhood, I saw a mailman running around biting dogs."

"There were 6,000 runners in the race. At least that's what they told me. It was hard for me to count them all . . . *they kept moving.* I'm glad they gave us numbers to wear on the front of our shirts. *It's hard to remember 6,000 names."*

"My friend Stan ran with me. Stan is getting married. We used to run together a lot, but you know when you get married you have to make some changes. Maybe give up a few things. So, Stan won't be running with me as much. Running isn't the only thing Stan had to give up. He won't be eating his favorite dessert anymore-custard. Stan loved custard, but his fiancee hated it. So, before he gave it up, she let him have one more bowl. It was *Stan's last custard!*"

"Someone else is getting married-my dog, Spot. Why not? Spot is a very smart dog. He can read and write. Last week he bought a car. When the loan officer at the bank got the paperwork ready, he told Spot to sign his name. Not only did he get the loan for the car, but it was the first time *Spot marked the X.*"

There, now you know why my name never gets mentioned in the same sentence with the likes of Jerry Lewis, Bob Hope, Henny Youngman, and Jay Leno. I tested my skills at stand-up comedy on amateur night in a club called Giggles. It was fun. Sometimes I received a polite applause and other times . . . well, let me put it this way. I never got good enough to give up my day job.

Even so, I have some serious thoughts about being funny. All across this country, any day of the week, there are support groups meeting to deal with almost every problem imaginable. In most cases, they begin their meetings with the Serenity prayer.

"God, grant me the serenity to accept the things I cannot change, the courage to change the things I can, and the wisdom to know the difference."

That prayer was written by Reinhold Niebuhr. I recently discovered this quote, also attributed to him. "Humor is a prelude to faith and laughter is the beginning of prayer."

On your *run to the Son,* make certain you pause at all the aid stations marked "laughter".

Mile 22
Crash, Boom,
Bang . . .

*"Let us come before
his presence with
thanksgiving and make
a joyful noise."*
Psalm 95:2

*She Loves You . . . I Want to Hold Your Hand . . . All My
Loving . . . Can't Buy Me Love . . . A Hard Day's Night . . . Help!
. . . Ticket to Ride . . . Hey Jude . . . Strawberry Fields . . .
Yesterday . . . The Long and Winding Road . . . Sergeant Pepper's
Lonely Heart's Club Band . . . Let It Be* . . . Thirty years after they
first invaded the airwaves, the Beatles, and their music, are still
there.

Just like most kids living in the USA, I was in front of the
television on that night in 1964 when Ed Sullivan introduced
them on his show. John, Paul, George, and Ringo, four young
men from Liverpool, England, counted down and kicked off into
their song, *All My Loving*.

Young girls screamed in admiration, adults shook their
heads in disdain, and legions of young men started growing their
hair long and learning how to strum the guitar. Cash registers
created a magic of their own, ringing up the sales of Beatles
records and other merchandise. Their influence was so great it
was reported that during that first appearance by the Beatles on
the Ed Sullivan show, not one crime was committed by a teen-
ager in New York City.

Like a lot of other kids, I wanted to be one of the Beatles. A school picture of me hung on the wall in our house and I didn't much care for it. One afternoon, when my mother wasn't around, I replaced it with a picture of John Lennon. I grew long hair and was criticized by teachers and other adults who, ironically, eventually gave into the winds of change and grew similar styles.

I collected Beatles trading cards and memorized the words to all their songs in my record collection. The Beatles were among the leaders and revolutionaries whose music and ideas sizzled throughout the sixties. I wanted to be just like them.

Strumming the guitar didn't turn out to be one of my gifts, so playing the drums and acting like Ringo became my specialty. There is an old Chinese proverb that says, "If you're mad at your neighbor, then buy your child a drum."

For years I tapped along to the Beatles' music with pencils, rolled up magazines, rulers, and other crude devices. Add a few pillows and cardboard boxes, a little imagination, and you've got a set of drums. After twenty-five years, something moved inside me. I had to have real drums-and I got them.

I bought a used set at a place called The Music Barn. Their motto is "No bull at the barn." Now I'm happy and I'm loud. Am I good? Well, shortly after setting up my new drum set, For Sale signs started appearing all over my neighborhood. Like I said-I'm happy and I'm loud.

Ringo may have set the tempo for the Beatles, but to set the tempo for your life, listen to the heartbeat of Jesus. *Keep running to the Son.*

Mile 23
The Great
Snidini

*"But seek ye first
the kingdom of God and
his righteousness; and all
these things shall be added
unto you."*
Matthew 6:33

"Hocus-pocus. Now you see it-now you don't. Ladies and gentleman, here to razzle-dazzle you with his spectacular assortment of magic tricks, is the one, the only, the incredible, the magnificent-*The Great Snidini!"*

Since my fortieth birthday rolled by a couple of years ago, I've felt an urgency to expand my horizons and try new things. Still to accomplish (and some I may forget about) are bungee jumping, alligator wrestling, bullfighting, being shot out of a cannon, going over Niagara Falls in a barrel, lion taming, sumo wrestling, running for president, and robbing a bank. As for now, *magic!*

The Columbus Metropolitan Library holds the distinction of being the first stop on this new adventure. Vanishing from their shelves by way of my library card were two books, *The Blackstone Book of Magic and Illusion*, by Harry Blackstone, and *The Encyclopedia of Magic and Magicians,* by T.A. Waters.

Before I eventually made these temporary acquisitions disappear into the darkness of the night-return box, I found out what abracadabra really means, how Harry Houdini did what he did, techniques for sawing my neighbor in half, and where to get a good deal on a magic wand.

It was time for a little practical application. Soon I was trooping up and down the aisles of a nearby toy store. My reconnaissance turned up three magic kits to choose from. I wrote a check for $9.51 and walked out of the store, the proud owner of the Marshall Brodien Magic Show (twelve magic tricks with a magician's table). It was designed for ages seven through adult. How could I go wrong?

Enthusiasm about my new vocation spilled over on the trip home. At the traffic light, I opened the box and dumped the contents on the seat beside me. My first trick was steering the car with my left hand, while using my right to examine a colorful assortment of boxes, balls, pins, and cards-all the while avoiding an accident.

A couple of days later, under the title of *The Great Snidini*, I was entertaining my family and friends with such remarkable feats as making a quarter vanish into a glass of water, poking holes in a cup without the contents leaking out, and producing a picture of a bunny rabbit on a tiny stick held in my hand-WOW-E-ZOWY!!!

Included with my magic kit was this advice, "Don't tell anyone how you do your tricks. Why spoil the fun? Be like a real magician-he never tells his secrets."

Of course, real life is not magic. We all have difficulties and heartaches that won't give up, no matter how many times we wave the magic wand.

Here is my advice, "No hocus-pocus, just stay focused on Jesus." *Keep running to the Son.*

90

Mile 24
The River

*"In the world ye
shall have tribulation: but
be of good cheer; I have
overcome the world."*
John 16:33

No, no and no. I don't work for a travel agency, I don't work for the West Virginia Chamber of Commerce, and I don't receive any honorarium for the following advertisement. But please, at least once in your lifetime, visit wild and wonderful West Virginia-and while you're there, go white water river rafting.

In the meantime, let me take you on a virtual reality rafting trip.

A qualified and friendly guide briefs us on the essentials of safety, then provides us with helmets, life jackets, and paddles. Now we're ready to stow our valuables in a dry bag, lash our lunch buckets down, and climb inside the raft. The crew of each raft consists of six to eight people and a guide with a total of five rafts to a group.

We're off. As we glide out to midriver, the guide makes sure every member of the crew is introduced to each other. With that last formality out of the way, we are ready for the serious business of having fun.

For the next several hours as we journey down the river, the crew will listen intently to the guide calling out our instructions: "Hard right, now everyone, fast forward . . . faster . . ."

We explode over the first rapid. Now the crew is soaked to the bone and the trip offers us a new perspective.

"Paddle gently now. Okay, coast for a moment-you can take off your helmets, if you wish."

Another boat glides into range as the guide completes his comments. In short order, there is a water battle underway as helmets become buckets.

"Helmets on, pick up your paddles. Straight ahead. Faster!"

This time, despite our best efforts to follow instructions, we lose two crew members over the side when we tumble into the next rapid. We safely retrieve them downstream, where the water smooths out. This scenario repeats itself several more times before we beach for lunch.

"Okay, get ready-here we go again!"

We plunge through several more rapids and everyone manages to stay in the boat. We will pause again to swim, jump off some tall rocks, then, back in the raft, glide downstream to the take-out point. Thanks to our guide, it's been a safe trip.

On the subject of men and rivers, Tolstoy wrote,

"One of the most widespread superstitions is that every man has his own special, definite qualities: That a man is kind, cruel, wise, stupid, energetic, apathetic, etc. Men are not like that. Men are like rivers-every river narrows here, is more rapid there, here slower, there broader, now clear, now cold, now dull, now warm. It is the same with men. Every man carries in himself the germs of every human quality, and sometimes,one manifests itself, sometimes another and the man often becomes unlike himself, while still remaining the same man."

I'm fortunate to have a one-on-one relationship with a qualified guide to help me on my journey through this life. He knows me, He knows the river.

You can know Him too. *Keep running to-Rafting with-* the Son.

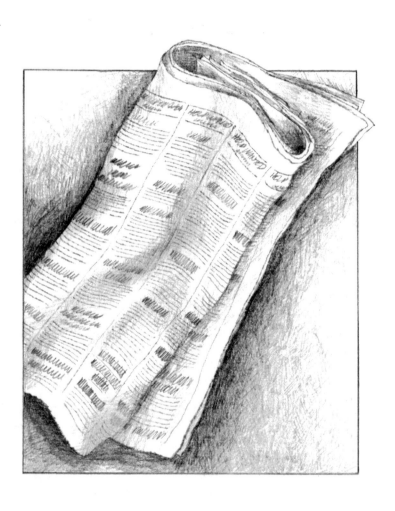

Mile 25
Hey, Look at Me!

*"I will instruct thee
and teach thee in the way
which thou shalt go: I will
guide thee with mine eye."*
Psalms 32:8

Someone told me about a study that concluded it took an average of 1,470 resumes to get one job. That's a lot of paper. So, obviously, the question is this: How do you get the people who are reading resumes to pull yours out of the stack first?

Here is what I did.

My goal: To obtain an entry level position on the creative staff of Mills/James Productions.

My plan began to take shape with a trip to the library and some help from a friend who teaches marketing at a local college. The idea was to learn as much about what goes on at Mills/James as I could.

After studying the material I gathered, the winds of good fortune began to blow my way again. While cruising the aisles of the supermarket, I noticed a man standing in line at the video rental. He was wearing a sweatshirt with Mills/James Productions boldly stitched across the front. Following a quick prayer (should I or shouldn't I?), I approached him.

I introduced myself and inquired about the opportunities to join his company. I discovered he was the operations manager and he was very kind to me, closing our conversation with a handshake and an invitation to send him a resume.

One week later, I left a voice mail message reminding him of our meeting in the supermarket. Next, I delivered to his office three boxes neatly bound together with string. Each box measured fourteen inches by ten inches and was two and one half inches deep. I placed a neatly typed two-page resume in each carton. Since Mills/James is in the business of video, film, and graphics, I knew I needed something extra. On the inside lid of box number one was a small poster reading, *I'd give the shirt off my back for a job at Mills/James* and, you guessed it, a T-shirt with the same message printed on it.

Box number two contained a poster that read, *I'd give my last dollar for a job at Mills/James.* The box was filled with large rolled up, wadded up, and loose reproductions of fifty, one hundred and one thousand dollar bills.

Hold on, there is one more box. Box number three contained a poster reading, *I'd go the extra mile for a job at Mills/James.* It also contained a five-by-seven picture of me crossing the finish line of a marathon race, some road maps, and a tiny pair of running shoes.

Do you think I got their attention?

Yes, I got their attention, an interview, compliments on my creativity and *a job!*

True, it's only a part-time job, but it's also the next opportunity to say, "Hey, look at me!"

While climbing the ladder of success or resting on the latest rung, you and I can take great comfort in the fact that we already have the attention of Jesus and if we want a place in his heart, no resume, interview or "Hey, look at me!" is required.

Just keep running to the Son.

Mile 26
Hell or High Water

*"Behold, we count
them happy which
endure."*
James 5:11

"I ran the Athens Marathon."

"Athens, Greece?"

"No, Athens, Ohio."

"How did you do?"

"There were seventy runners in the race and I beat all but sixty-nine of them."

"You beat all but sixty-nine of them? That means you came in last. Bet you felt like a fool."

"No, I didn't feel like a fool. In fact, I was rather proud of myself."

"How so?"

"Because I know what the strongest nation in the world is."

"What does that have to do with running a marathon race?"

"It has everything to do with it. Now you answer the question. What is the strongest nation in the world?"

"The United States."

"No."

"Japan."

"No."

"You're wasting my time."

"Okay, I'll tell you what the strongest nation in the world is. It's *determination.*"

"That was a trick question."

"Not really, if you think about it."

"You're nuts."

"Let me tell you a story about a flood."

"What does a flood have to do with a marathon race?"

"You'll see."

"I can't wait."

"There was this flood, and as floods go, it was a pretty bad one. The rain was coming down in buckets, the dam had broken lose and the water was rising fast. People were in a panic. There was no time to save anything but your life. People were on the roofs of their houses, crying, shouting and praying for help. Suddenly, their attention became riveted on a hat."

"A hat?"

"Yes, a hat. It was going back and forth in the water in front of the houses. It was very strange to watch. It just kept going back and forth in straight lines."

"What made it do that?"

"The people were pointing to the hat now. It had everyone's attention. They were shouting, 'What is it? What is it'?"

"Okay, you got me. What happened next?"

"A lady on the rooftop of one of the houses stood up and told everyone to relax. The hat belonged to her husband who had said that today, *come hell or high water,* he was going to cut the grass."

"Your point being?"

"That's *DETERMINATION.*"

"What about the marathon?"

"It was tough. There were lots of hills. I mean big ones that mountain goats wouldn't even climb."

"I think you're putting me on."

"I had a hard time. I got sick and fell behind the rest of

102

the group. I kept going, even though I had to walk about five miles."

"Why didn't you quit?"

"Something inside me said, 'Don't give up. You can do it'."

"And you did."

"I got my strength back and decided to run the last mile. When I passed the twenty-six mile marker, I paused long enough to pull it out of the ground."

"Then what did you do?"

"I carried it in my hand like an Olympic torch as I ran for the finish line."

"Congratulations!"

"I've run thirty marathons now, and Athens was the toughest. It is also the one I'm most proud of."

"Why?"

"When you focus on Jesus and not the race, you'll always win."

Keep running to the Son.

103

Mile 26.2
And Then
Some

*"And whoever shall
compel you to do one mile,
go with him two."*
Matthew 5:41

Not many people will spend time debating whether or not twenty-six miles is a long way to run. It *is* a long way indeed. If you happen to be running a marathon race, even after you've run twenty-six miles, you're still not finished. An official marathon race is 26.2 miles long.

"Why 26.2 miles?" you ask.

The marathon race got its start in ancient Greece. There, in the year 490 B.C., a man named Pheidippies ran twenty-six miles from the plains of Marathon to Athens. His mission was to announce a military victory over the Persian army.

"Victory is ours! Athens is saved!" he shouted as he completed the run. For an encore, he collapsed and died.

Surprisingly, the sport of marathon running did not end with the death of its first participant. The first Olympic Games were held in 1896 and the agenda included a race between the cities of Marathon and Athens. The distance of the race underwent several changes until the 1924 Olympic Games. At that time, it was set at twenty-six miles, 385 yards-or 26.2 miles. It has remained so ever since. Now we're back to your original question, "Why 26.2 miles?"

When the games were being held in London, several modifications to the marathon race course were made in order to please the royal family. By the time race officials were done making adjustments to the start and finish lines, and the king and his court were situated to watch the race from the comfort of their castle, it turned out to be 26.2 miles.

Now you know. Because of a royal request, marathon runners go twenty-six miles and then some.

Think about that phrase, *and then some*. Have you ever known an *and then some* person? More importantly, have you ever considered yourself to be an *and then some* person? You won't find the definition in the dictionary, so let me explain what I think it means.

And then some people . . .

• Take the extra time to send you a card, make a telephone call, listen to your troubles, or just be there.

• Spend a little extra money to buy flowers, a book of encouragement, or a teddy bear.

• Choose their words carefully and make sure they sprinkle in extra compliments and words of appreciation when cooking up a conversation.

• Give extra effort in a relationship. They listen with their heart. They listen for feelings.

• Know how to forgive and make that extra effort to bury the hatchet without marking the grave.

Without question, the all time greatest *and then some person* is Jesus. Nearly 2,000 years ago, He died on the cross for you and me. More importantly-He came back.

Now, and forevermore . . .

Run to the Son,
Jerry Snider